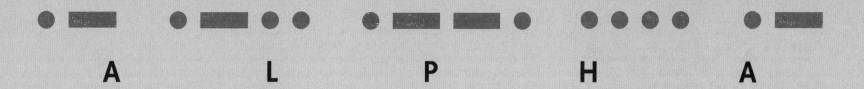

A L P H A

B R A V O

C H A R L I E

This book floated across the ocean in a cardboard box, inside a metal container, on a very big ship. I dedicate it to those at sea who make it possible for books to travel great distances into the hands of children.

Just like a ship, every book has a crew. I am deeply grateful to:

Captain John Dickinson of The Nautical Institute, who opened my eyes to the hidden world of ships and boats, and shared his invaluable expertise gained over many years at sea.

Meagan Bennett, Maya Gartner and Cecily Kaiser at Phaidon, who brilliantly inspired ALPHA, BRAVO, CHARLIE, and provided impeccable vision, talent and support.

Lea Edgar, Librarian/Archivist at the Vancouver Maritime Museum; Natasha Brown of the International Maritime Organization; and Dr Rachel Poliquin, Writer and Curator, who provided critical resources and careful research.

My family, who helped me research beautiful boats and flags everywhere on our beloved Sunshine Coast.

Every other hand, on land or at sea, who helped to make and deliver this book.

Phaidon Press Limited
Regent's Wharf
All Saints Street
London, N1 9PA

phaidon.com

First published 2016
© 2016 Phaidon Press Limited
Text and illustration copyright © Sara Gillingham

Text set in Super Grotesk

ISBN 978 0 7148 7125 7 (UK edition)
008-1215

Designed by Meagan Bennett
Text support by Sarah Hutt

Printed in China

ALPHA, BRAVO, CHARLIE
The Complete Book of Nautical Codes

by SARA GILLINGHAM

INTRODUCTION

Ship Ahoy!

Imagine you are on a boat at sea, a long time ago, with no phone or electronic way to talk to anyone else. Sailing in the big, wide ocean is pretty dangerous! There are pirate ships that could rob you, and maybe even enemy ships from countries you are at war with.

So when you see another ship in the distance, what do you do? Are the people aboard friends or enemies? The only tool you have is a small telescope. You raise it to your eye and bring the ship into view. There, flying high in the air, is a bright, colourful flag that sends you important information about that ship. This flag is called a SIGNAL FLAG!

What Are Signal Flags?

When pirates used to sail the seas looking for treasure to steal, the grinning white skull of their pirate flag was a clear and frightening way for them to tell far-off ships what they wanted. Signal flags work in much the same way. They use a combination of five bold colours, arranged in simple shapes and patterns, to send visual messages across great distances. The flags

were created by sailors and have been used for hundreds of years. Today they are an important part of the International Code of Signals, a special language used by sailors in over 170 different countries!

How Do Signal Flags Work?

Signal flags are a code that all sailors must learn. There are forty flags in total, but the most well-known ones are the twenty-six alphabet flags – one for each letter. Those flags can be used to spell out words. More importantly, each flag also has its own meaning when it's flown by itself. In other words, sailors can fly a single flag, like the N flag, which by itself means "No" or "Negative". Or they can signal an urgent message like "Man Overboard" (O flag) or "You Are Running Into Danger" (U flag). These single flag meanings let passing ships know quickly if there is an important instruction, an emergency or a need for help.

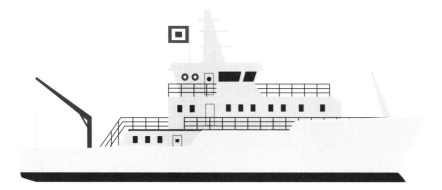

Phonetic Alphabet

When sailors talk about the flags or decoding any kind of message, they don't just say the name of letters. Instead they use the International Radiotelephony Spelling Alphabet, or, the Phonetic Alphabet for short. This alphabet matches each letter with a word, so anyone reading a code out loud can't mix up similar-sounding letters. For example, if you say the letter "d" someone may mistake it for "b" or "p", so instead, you would say "D as in Delta" or just "Delta." In this special alphabet, A, B and C become Alpha, Bravo and Charlie.

Morse Code

What about when it's cloudy or it's night-time, and sailors can't see signal flags? Morse code is a system that treats letters of the alphabet as combinations of dits (short tones) and dahs (long tones). For example: A is one dit and one dah. Sailors can send Morse signals with light (using a blinking lamp), or by sound (using radio) when signal flags won't work.

Semaphore

Semaphore is another way that sailors used to send messages in the past. Each letter of the alphabet is represented by a person holding a set of two matching flags in a certain position. For example:

A   B   C   D   E   F   G

A is signalled by holding your left arm straight down and your right arm out at a downward angle. Semaphore lets sailors spell out messages very quickly, which used to be very handy when ships were close to each other.

Why Are These Signals Important?

Ships are still very important to the way we live today. Almost everything we use is brought to us by sea! Without ships, items such as clothing, paper, toys, furniture, cars and so much more would never make it to our towns and shops. Even though sailors have modern ways of talking to each other these days, sometimes those tools fail, or ships enter areas where they cannot use them. That's when these original codes of the sea save the day!

Using This Book

So, are YOU ready to learn how to signal? For every letter of the alphabet, this book features the associated signal flag, the Phonetic Alphabet word, the Morse code and the semaphore sign. You will learn four different nautical languages! Each letter also features an illustration and a short description of a type of boat. In the back of the book, there is a glossary of terms that explains what some nautical words mean, and a list of websites you can look at to learn even more. It's everything you need to become an expert!

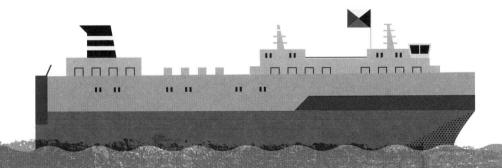

FLAG LETTER:	FLAG MEANING:
# A	# I HAVE A DIVER DOWN; KEEP WELL CLEAR AT LOW SPEED.
FLAG NAME: **ALPHA**	

When you see the ALPHA flag, it means a scuba diver is under the water. Lots of people dive for fun, but a ship's crew often sends divers deep down into the ocean to work: inspecting ships, making repairs, or even looking for things from wrecked ships!

When a diver goes underwater, it's important for nearby ships to know because the spinning blades of a passing ship's propeller are also underwater and can be very dangerous. It's also important because a boat with a diver down may not be able to move out of the way to avoid a crash.

Any boat that sees an ALPHA flag should slow down and give the ship lots of space, to keep divers and diving boats safe.

OTHER NAUTICAL CODES FOR THE LETTER "A"

PHONETIC ALPHABET

ALPHA is pronounced al-fah. Other military and phonetic alphabets have used Apples, Ack, Ace and Able.

MORSE CODE / SOUND AND LIGHT SIGNAL

Make one short tone and one long tone.

SEMAPHORE

With your left arm pointing straight down, hold your right arm out at a downward diagonal.

ABOUT DIVING BOATS

A diving boat can come in many different shapes and sizes, but there must be room for divers' tanks and safety equipment, and a ladder for divers to climb on and off the boat.

FLAG LETTER:

B

FLAG NAME:
BRAVO

FLAG MEANING:

I AM CARRYING DANGEROUS CARGO.

Did you know that ships bring to us many of the things we use every day, like clothes, books and food from other countries around the world? But this cargo, which is the word for things that are transported by ship, can sometimes be toxic, explosive or very dangerous if handled incorrectly. For example, oil is a very dangerous type of cargo because of the damage it can cause to humans and animals if it spills.

That's why ships fly the BRAVO flag – it warns other ships that there is "dangerous cargo" aboard. It also tells the other boats that they must give the ship a "wide berth", meaning they steer clear of the ship and give it lots of extra space. But what about at night when it's hard to see the flag? When a ship with dangerous cargo is in a harbour at night, it will often shine a red warning light to let nearby boats know to stay well away.

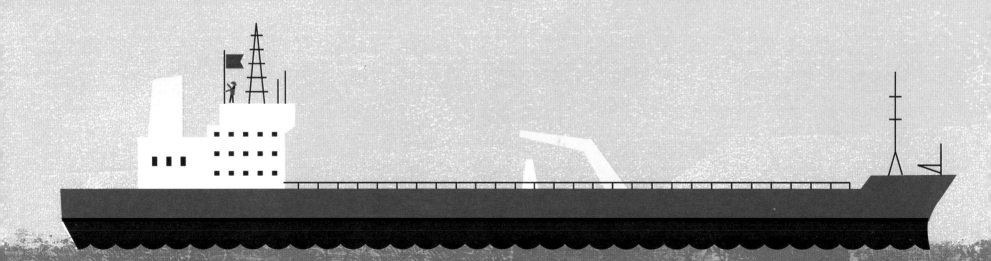

OTHER NAUTICAL CODES FOR THE LETTER "B"

PHONETIC ALPHABET

BRAVO

BRAVO is pronounced brah-voh. Other military and phonetic alphabets have used Butter, Beer and Baker.

MORSE CODE / SOUND AND LIGHT SIGNAL

Make one long tone and three short tones with equal space between them.

SEMAPHORE

With your left arm pointing straight down to your side, hold your right arm straight out to the right.

ABOUT OIL TANKERS

An oil tanker carries large amounts of oil across very long distances. The oil is carried within massive tanks inside the ship, and once the ship arrives, the oil is moved off the tanker through a hose.

FLAG LETTER:

C

FLAG NAME:
CHARLIE

FLAG MEANING:

YES or AFFIRMATIVE.

Aye aye, Captain. That's one way to answer yes. Another way is to fly the CHARLIE flag. Let's say one ship has a problem with its radio and it stops sending radio messages.

A nearby ship asks, "Is your radio not working?" The ship with the broken radio can raise the CHARLIE flag to answer "Affirmative" or "Yes". The two ships can then use signal flags or Morse code to keep communicating and solve the problem.

OTHER NAUTICAL CODES FOR THE LETTER "C"

PHONETIC ALPHABET

CHARLIE

CHARLIE is pronounced char-lee. This word has been used for C in all kinds of military and phonetic alphabets, so it must work well!

MORSE CODE / SOUND AND LIGHT SIGNAL

Make one long tone, one short tone, one long tone, one short tone, with equal space between them.

SEMAPHORE

With your left arm pointing straight down, hold your right arm out at an upward diagonal.

ABOUT SAILBOATS

A sailboat moves with the natural power of wind and sails, so it doesn't usually need a motor or fuel once it gets going. Sailors move the sails to make the wind push the boat in the right direction.

FLAG LETTER:

D

FLAG NAME:
DELTA

FLAG MEANING:

KEEP CLEAR OF ME; I AM MANOEUVRING WITH DIFFICULTY.

Tugboats can push cargo as well as tug (or pull) it. When a tugboat is pushing a very heavy boat, it is "manoeuvring with difficulty", which means that it is not able to move as quickly or steer as well as it normally does, so it is safer for other boats to stay away. For example, tugboats often push big barges, which are boats that carry goods but can't move in the water without help. This would be the right time for the tugboat to fly the DELTA flag, telling other ships to keep a good distance, because it would be difficult for the tugboat to make a quick stop and avoid crashing.

OTHER NAUTICAL CODES FOR THE LETTER "D"

PHONETIC ALPHABET

DELTA is pronounced dell-tah. Other military and phonetic alphabets have used Duff, Don and Dog.

MORSE CODE / SOUND AND LIGHT SIGNAL

Make one long tone and two short tones with equal space between them.

SEMAPHORE

With your left arm pointing straight down, hold your right arm straight up.

ABOUT TUGBOATS

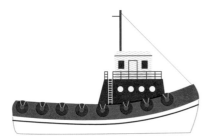

A tugboat is a superstrong boat that is able to push or pull other boats, barges or floating platforms that aren't able to move in water by themselves.

FLAG LETTER: # E **FLAG NAME:** **ECHO**	**FLAG MEANING:** # I AM ALTERING MY COURSE TO STARBOARD. (I AM TURNING RIGHT.)

Did you know that on a ship, left and right are called something totally different? When you are on board facing the front of the boat, left is called PORT. That's the side that ships use for docking in a port, when loading and offloading things. Right is known as STARBOARD. This comes from an Old English word, steorbord, which was a special oar used for steering on the right side of old-fashioned ships.

When a ship wants to pass another ship on the starboard side, the first ship raises the ECHO flag. It can also sound the ECHO signal, with one short blast (which is the same as E in Morse code). Either way, ECHO lets a nearby boat know which way the ship is turning, like a car indicator, to avoid crashes. And that's always a good thing!

OTHER NAUTICAL CODES FOR THE LETTER "E"

PHONETIC ALPHABET

ECHO

ECHO is pronounced eck-oh. Other military and phonetic alphabets have used Edward and Easy (which is Easy to remember!).

MORSE CODE / SOUND AND LIGHT SIGNAL

Make one short tone.

SEMAPHORE

With your right arm pointing straight down, hold your left arm out to the left at an upward angle.

ABOUT YACHTS

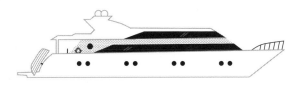

A yacht is any boat that is designed for pleasure rather than work, and has a living space inside. A yacht can be powered by sail or motor, or both.

FLAG LETTER:	FLAG MEANING:
# F	## I AM DISABLED; COMMUNICATE WITH ME.
FLAG NAME: **FOXTROT**	

Have you ever seen a broken-down car by the side of the road? It flashes its hazard lights to warn other cars that it has stopped, and to signal that it needs help. For a ship, flying the FOXTROT flag is the same thing. This flag tells other boats that the ship is not working properly, for example, if a log gets stuck in its motor!

But there's more. It also asks other boats to stop and communicate with the troubled ship in order to help.

If a captain or crew sees a FOXTROT flag flying, they will try and make contact with the ship in distress by using radio, hoisting a flag, or using Morse code with a signal lamp to find out how they can help.

OTHER NAUTICAL CODES FOR THE LETTER "F"

PHONETIC ALPHABET

FOXTROT

FOXTROT is pronounced foks-trot. This unusual word is also the name of a dance step! Other military and phonetic alphabets have used Freddie and Fox.

MORSE CODE / SOUND AND LIGHT SIGNAL

Make two short tones, one long tone and one short tone, with equal space between them.

SEMAPHORE

With your right arm pointing straight down, hold your left arm straight out beside you.

ABOUT FISHING BOATS

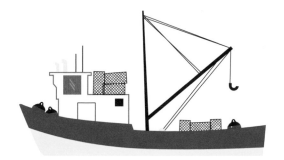

A fishing boat comes in many different shapes and sizes, depending on what kind of fish it is designed to catch and where it is fishing. A commercial fishing boat is any boat or ship that catches fish or seafood to sell.

FLAG MEANING:

I REQUIRE A PILOT.

Most harbours require ships to use a pilot when docking, which is when a boat is brought into harbour and "parked" in the right position. This pilot isn't the same as the person who flies an aeroplane. A nautical pilot is an expert who knows local waters and can help steer a ship through dangerous or tricky passages. If a ship does not have a pilot on board, the GOLF flag is a quick way to signal for one. Once it's raised, a pilot is sent from shore on a small high-speed pilot boat or sometimes even flown in by helicopter!

PHONETIC ALPHABET

GOLF is pronounced golf. Other military and phonetic alphabets have used George and Gee.

MORSE CODE / SOUND AND LIGHT SIGNAL

Make two long tones and one short tone with equal space between them.

SEMAPHORE

With your right arm pointing straight down, hold your left arm out beside you at a downward diagonal.

ABOUT PILOT BOATS

A pilot boat is a strong, fast boat that is usually painted a bright colour to make it easy to spot. It is used to transport pilots between land and the ship that needs piloting.

FLAG LETTER:

H

FLAG NAME:
HOTEL

FLAG MEANING:

I HAVE A PILOT ON BOARD.

Following the GOLF flag, the HOTEL flag is raised to let other boats and harbour officials know that a pilot is on board and is controlling the ship. This flag is raised after the pilot arrives at the ship and makes it on board. But that's not always easy.

When a pilot arrives by pilot boat, he or she has to climb up the side of the ship on a special pilot ladder made of wood (or aluminium) and rope. This ladder is built very carefully to remain stable and straight (without twisting) in all weather conditions.

Even so, climbing the pilot ladder can be very dangerous. Just imagine climbing a tree while the branches are moving – it's tricky! Once on board, pilots are expected to manoeuvre large ships through challenging waters. This is why pilots are special crew members. They're trusted with very important and sometimes unsafe jobs.

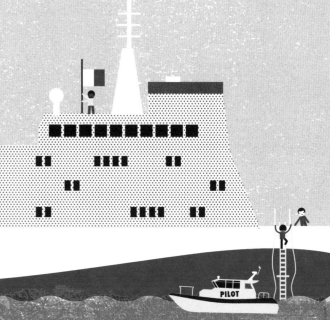

OTHER NAUTICAL CODES FOR THE LETTER "H"

PHONETIC ALPHABET

HOTEL is pronounced hoh-tel. Other military and phonetic alphabets have used Harry and How.

MORSE CODE / SOUND AND LIGHT SIGNAL

Make four short tones with equal space between them.

SEMAPHORE

With your right arm pointing straight out beside you, cross your left arm over your front and hold it under your right arm at a downward diagonal.

ABOUT JUICE TANKERS

A juice tanker is like an oil tanker, but instead of big tanks of oil, it is filled with big tanks of fruit juice! The juice is delivered to a packing house where it is packaged and delivered to shops.

FLAG LETTER:

I

FLAG NAME:
INDIA

FLAG MEANING:

I AM ALTERING MY COURSE TO PORT. (I AM TURNING LEFT.)

When you ride your bike and want to turn left, you stick out your left arm to signal. Well, on a ship when a sailor plans to veer left (or to "port"), the INDIA flag is raised to say "I am altering my course to port". Boats with sound signals can also use Morse code by giving two blasts.

Here's a way to remember left (port) from right (starboard) at sea. For port, you can say, "A ship that is sailing out to the ocean has 'left port'". For starboard, say, "Star light, star bright, starboard is to the right".

At night, sailors have yet another way to tell left from right. Navigation lights are used to help other boats know which side is which. A red light is used for the port side and a green light is used for starboard.

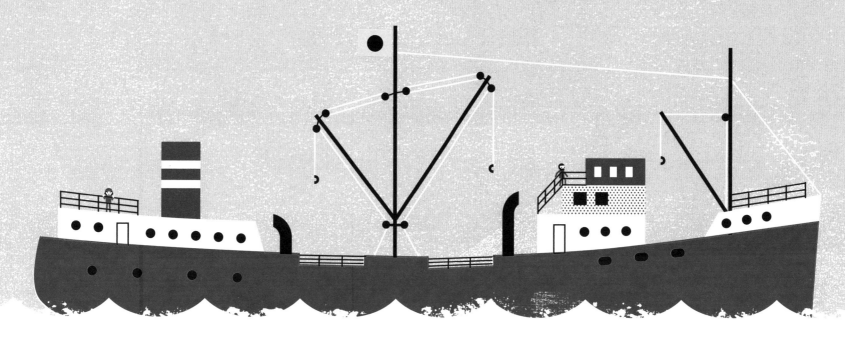

PHONETIC ALPHABET

INDIA is pronounced in-dee-ah. Other military and phonetic alphabets have used Ink and Item.

SEMAPHORE

With your right arm pointing at an upward angle beside you, cross your left arm over your front and out under your right arm at a downward angle.

MORSE CODE / SOUND AND LIGHT SIGNAL

Make two short tones.

ABOUT COASTAL SHIPS

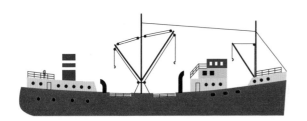

Coastal ships are smaller than tankers, and are used to deliver goods around the same continent or island. Their hull, or bottom, is not as deep as a tanker – which means they can go to places that bigger ships cannot.

J

FLAG MEANING:

I AM ON FIRE AND HAVE DANGEROUS CARGO ON BOARD: KEEP WELL CLEAR OF ME.

No sailor wants to fly the JULIET flag. This flag is only used when there is serious trouble on board. It tells other ships to alert the authorities and to stay far away, especially when there is explosive or toxic cargo on board. A sailor might hoist the JULIET flag when a fire has damaged the radio or electronics, making it impossible to communicate. If crew members can't put out the fire, the next step after raising the flag is to put on life jackets and evacuate (leave) the ship!

OTHER NAUTICAL CODES FOR THE LETTER "J"

PHONETIC ALPHABET

JULIET

JULIET is pronounced jew-lee-ett, like the character in Shakespeare's *Romeo and Juliet*. Other military and phonetic alphabets have used Johnnie and Jig.

MORSE CODE / SOUND AND LIGHT SIGNAL

Make one short tone and three long tones with equal space between them.

SEMAPHORE

With your right arm pointing straight up, hold your left arm straight out beside you.

ABOUT CARGO SHIPS

A cargo ship is a very large boat, usually made of steel and often equipped with cranes. It is designed to carry large quantities of goods from one port to another.

FLAG MEANING:

I WISH TO COMMUNICATE WITH YOU.

Raising this flag is almost like waving hello. Sailors raise the KILO flag when they want to communicate with another ship. The ships can continue to communicate using flag codes, but sometimes they decide to use other codes. They let each other know how they would like to communicate by adding a number flag underneath the KILO flag.

There are 10 number flags, each representing the numbers zero to nine. Four of them are used with the KILO flag. If a sailor wants to communicate by hand-flag, he indicates this by hoisting the KILO flag with the number one flag. If he wants to communicate using a loud hailer or megaphone, he signals this by hoisting the KILO flag with the number two flag. He can also hoist the number three flag for Morse lamp and the four flag for sound signals.

OTHER NAUTICAL CODES FOR THE LETTER "K"

PHONETIC ALPHABET

KILO

KILO is pronounced key-loh. Other military and phonetic alphabets have used King.

MORSE CODE / SOUND AND LIGHT SIGNAL

Make one long tone, one short tone and one long tone, with equal space between them.

SEMAPHORE

With your left arm pointing straight up, hold your right arm out at a downward angle beside you.

ABOUT PATROL BOATS

A patrol boat is used by the coastguard to keep an eye out for dangerous or illegal activity so those at sea and in coastal areas can stay safe – just like a patrol car!

FLAG LETTER:

L

FLAG NAME:
LIMA

FLAG MEANING:

YOU SHOULD STOP YOUR VESSEL INSTANTLY.

STOP! That's the message sailors get loud and clear when they see the LIMA flag flying. A ship can use this flag to warn a nearby boat when the boat is heading towards something dangerous, like an underwater reef. Port officials also use this flag to order a vessel (which is another word for a large boat or ship) to stop in a busy harbour. But most of the time, they use the Morse code sound signal to instantly alert a ship that it needs to stop.

OTHER NAUTICAL CODES FOR THE LETTER "L"

PHONETIC ALPHABET

LIMA is pronounced lee-mah. Other military and phonetic alphabets have used London and Love.

MORSE CODE / SOUND AND LIGHT SIGNAL

Make one short tone, one long tone and two short tones, with equal space between them.

SEMAPHORE

With your left arm pointing at an upward angle, hold your right arm at a downward angle beside you.

ABOUT POLICE BOATS

A police boat is a fast boat used by the police to help enforce (make people obey) the law at sea. Police boats are important in bigger ports, where there are many boats and people coming and going.

FLAG LETTER:

M

FLAG NAME:
MIKE

FLAG MEANING:

MY VESSEL IS STOPPED AND MAKING NO WAY THROUGH THE WATER.

Sometimes, it can be difficult to tell if a far-away boat is moving in the water. "Making no way" means that a boat is not moving, and it's important for nearby ships to know this so that they don't bump into it. So a boat should let other ships know that they have stopped by hoisting the MIKE flag. This way, other ships know to move around them.

OTHER NAUTICAL CODES FOR THE LETTER "M"

PHONETIC ALPHABET

MIKE

MIKE is pronounced mike. Other military and phonetic alphabets have used Monkey and even Emma (for the m's in the middle!).

MORSE CODE / SOUND AND LIGHT SIGNAL

Make two long tones.

SEMAPHORE

With your right arm pointing out beside you at a downward diagonal, hold your left arm straight out beside you.

ABOUT ICEBREAKERS

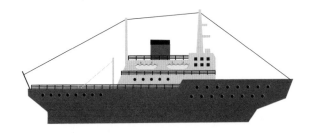

An icebreaker is a powerful boat with a very strong and specially-shaped hull, or bottom, that can break paths through solid ice when the ocean is frozen. These paths help other boats sail to places that they otherwise would not be able to reach.

FLAG MEANING:

NO or NEGATIVE.

N stands for "No!" The NOVEMBER flag should be hoisted if a sailor's reply to a signal is "No", or if a crew is unable to do what another boat is asking them to.

Did you know that many of the flags in this book can be combined to send a completely different message? One very important flag combination is NOVEMBER and CHARLIE (the "Yes" flag). When these flags are hoisted together, it becomes an urgent signal for help, just like S-O-S in Morse code. These signals are only used for big emergencies, like sinking ships, or if someone is very hurt.

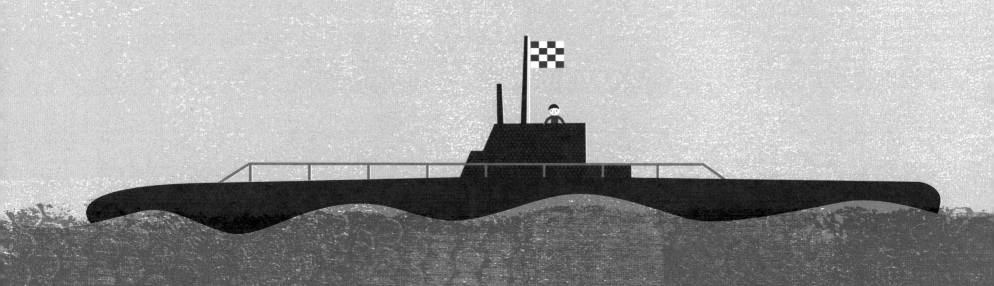

OTHER NAUTICAL CODES FOR THE LETTER "N"

PHONETIC ALPHABET

NOVEMBER

NOVEMBER is pronounced no-vem-ber. Other military and phonetic alphabets have used Nuts, Nab and Nan.

MORSE CODE / SOUND AND LIGHT SIGNAL

Make one long tone and one short tone.

SEMAPHORE

Hold both your arms out beside you at a downward angle.

ABOUT SUBMARINES

A submarine is designed to manoeuvre completely underwater. It is often painted a dark, unshiny colour or in camouflage, so that it is hard to see in the water and can be sneaky.

FLAG LETTER:

O

FLAG NAME:
OSCAR

FLAG MEANING:

MAN OVERBOARD.

"Man Overboard!" is what crew members and passengers shout if someone falls into the water from a ship. This is a serious situation and can be deadly if help doesn't get there fast. To alert nearby boats, sailors raise the OSCAR flag.

Man Overboard signals should then be sent out by flag, radio, smoke, horn or whatever is available on the boat so that nearby ships can offer help. Things that help people float, like lifebelts (ring-shaped tubes that are used to help keep people from drowning), are always kept on boats for just this reason. Ladders, rope, fabric, bare hands and even waves can be used to help the person get back on to the boat. With quick thinking and fast action, people who fall overboard can be saved.

OTHER NAUTICAL CODES FOR THE LETTER "O"

PHONETIC ALPHABET

OSCAR

OSCAR is pronounced oss-cah. Other military and phonetic alphabets have used Orange and Oboe.

MORSE CODE / SOUND AND LIGHT SIGNAL

Make three long tones with equal space between them.

SEMAPHORE

Hold your right arm out beside you at an upward diagonal, with your left arm crossed over your front and straight out under your right arm.

ABOUT AIRCRAFT CARRIERS

An aircraft carrier is a huge naval ship with a landing strip for aircrafts to take off and land on. It is the most important ship in the navy, because it allows troops to have a home base anywhere in the world.

FLAG LETTER:

P

FLAG NAME:
PAPA

ALL PERSONS SHOULD REPORT ON BOARD: PROCEEDING TO SEA or MY NETS HAVE COME FAST UPON AN OBSTRUCTION.

When a ship is in the harbour, having the PAPA flag flying is like the conductor of a train shouting "All Aboard". It means that all passengers or crew on shore should board the ship, because it is about to leave! The PAPA flag is also called the Departure Flag, and is normally hoisted 24 hours before departure (leaving).

When a fishing boat is at sea, the PAPA flag is hoisted in order to let other ships know that their underwater nets are caught on something, like jagged rocks or a sunken shipwreck. A boat with snagged nets can be very dangerous because the nets can get so tangled up that the ship capsizes (turns over). Even when things are under control, nets are very expensive, so fishing boats try to move around, to carefully free them without damage. Other ships should keep clear when they see the PAPA flag, unless the fishing boat specifically asks for help.

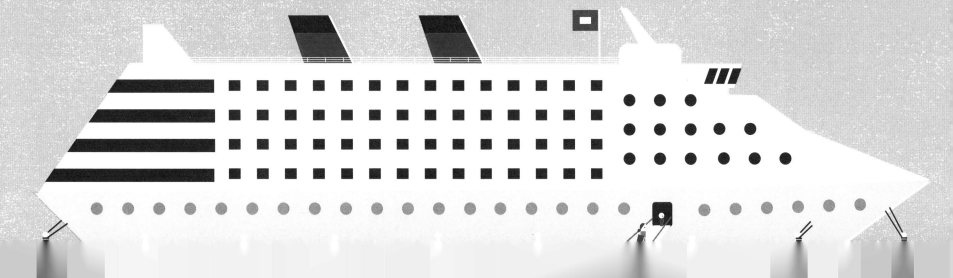

OTHER NAUTICAL CODES FOR THE LETTER "P"

PHONETIC ALPHABET

PAPA

PAPA is pronounced pah-pah. Other military and phonetic alphabets have used Pudding, Pip, Peter and Prep.

SEMAPHORE

Hold your right arm straight out beside you, and your left arm straight up.

MORSE CODE / SOUND AND LIGHT SIGNAL

Make one short tone, two long tones and one short tone, with equal space between them.

ABOUT CRUISE SHIPS

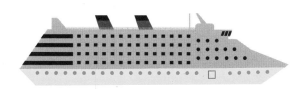

A cruise ship is a large boat that takes big groups of passengers to exciting places. There are sleeping cabins (like hotel rooms) on board, and many cruise ships have swimming pools, restaurants and performers!

FLAG LETTER:

Q

FLAG NAME:
QUEBEC

FLAG MEANING:

MY VESSEL IS HEALTHY AND I REQUEST FREE PRATIQUE.

To "request free pratique" means to ask for permission to dock in someone else's port. If a boat is flying the QUEBEC flag when it enters port, an official from the port will usually come on board and request to see medical papers proving that everyone on the boat is healthy. This is an important way to control the spread of deadly diseases.

But this wasn't always the case. A long time ago, flying the QUEBEC flag meant that your ship was in quarantine. This is when one person or more on the ship is very ill with a contagious disease and the ship has to drop anchor and keep everyone on board to stop the illness from spreading.

OTHER NAUTICAL CODES FOR THE LETTER "Q"

PHONETIC ALPHABET

QUEBEC

QUEBEC is pronounced keh-beck. The name is also a province in Canada. Other military and phonetic alphabets have used Queen and Queenie.

SEMAPHORE

Hold your right arm straight out, and your left arm at an upward angle.

MORSE CODE / SOUND AND LIGHT SIGNAL

Make two long tones, one short tone and one long tone, with equal space between them.

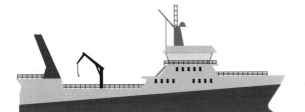

ABOUT LARGE FACTORY SHIPS

A factory ship is a very big fishing boat that has special equipment on board so that it can keep the fish that it catches fresh for the whole time it is at sea.

FLAG MEANING:

[THERE IS NO FLAG MEANING!]

The ROMEO flag is unique because it doesn't have a meaning any more. In older versions of the code, it used to mean "Do not pass ahead of me". But today, it simply stands for the letter R and is only used when sailors want to spell out words with that letter, or send a message in combination with other flags. For example, it is used with number flags to help sailors talk about the distance between ships or between ship and port. It is also used with other alphabet flags for more detailed messages about anchoring, which is when a ship drops a heavy metal anchor into the water to help it stay in one place.

The Morse signal for R is one short tone, one long tone and one short tone, and is often used by a ship anchored in fog, which makes it very hard to see! The sound signal lets other boats know that the ship is there so that they don't crash into the ship!

PHONETIC ALPHABET

ROMEO

ROMEO is pronounced row-me-oh, just like in Shakespeare's *Romeo and Juliet*. Other military and phonetic alphabets have used Robert and Roger.

MORSE CODE / SOUND AND LIGHT SIGNAL

Make one short tone, one long tone and one short tone, with equal space between them.

SEMAPHORE

Hold both of your arms straight out beside you.

ABOUT CLIPPERS

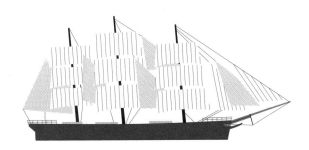

A clipper ship is a big, fast, wooden sailboat that was especially popular in the 1800s. Today they are used mostly for fun, but long ago, clippers were used for bringing large amounts of things like tea, spices, wool and gold from one place to another.

FLAG LETTER:

S

FLAG NAME:
SIERRA

I AM OPERATING ASTERN PROPULSION.

A boat is "operating astern propulsion" when it is slowing down or backing up. It is difficult to see when a boat is operating astern propulsion, since it doesn't make a wave or tracks in the water. That's why it's important to warn other boats so that they can steer clear.

The SIERRA flag is used only in cases where there is no other communication on a boat due to radio silence or broken equipment. The more common way to send this signal is by sound. The sound signal for SIERRA is the Morse code for S: three short blasts. This is a sound you hear often in ports today.

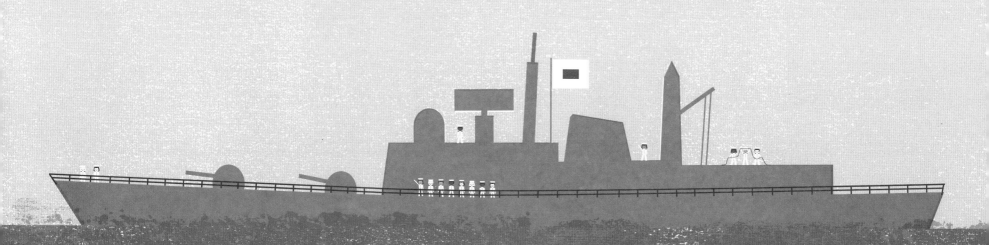

OTHER NAUTICAL CODES FOR THE LETTER "S"

PHONETIC ALPHABET

SIERRA is pronounced see-air-rah. Other military and phonetic alphabets have used Sugar.

MORSE CODE / SOUND AND LIGHT SIGNAL

Make three short tones with equal space between them.

SEMAPHORE

Hold your right arm straight out beside you, and your left arm at a downward diagonal.

ABOUT DESTROYERS

A destroyer is a fast and agile naval ship that can protect larger, slower-moving ships against submarines and aircrafts.

T

FLAG MEANING:

KEEP CLEAR OF ME; I AM ENGAGED IN PAIR TRAWLING.

The tango is a complicated dance between two people. The TANGO flag is used to indicate a complicated movement that two ships make together. Though it's not flown very often any more, when it is, it means that a boat is pair trawling – a type of fishing where two boats tow a huge fishing net between them. With pair trawling, fishermen can use a bigger net than they would be able to by themselves, but this also means that other boats need to keep clear so they don't get tangled up in the net or scare away the fish.

Pair trawling makes some people very angry because of the amount of ocean life that it destroys or catches by mistake. So these days, it's actually not allowed in some places.

OTHER NAUTICAL CODES FOR THE LETTER "T"

PHONETIC ALPHABET

TANGO is pronounced tang-go. Other military and phonetic alphabets have used Tommy, Toc and Tare.

MORSE CODE / SOUND AND LIGHT SIGNAL

Make one long tone.

SEMAPHORE

Hold your left arm straight up above your head, and your right arm at an upward diagonal.

ABOUT TRAWLERS

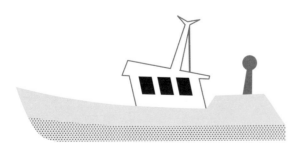

A trawler (sometimes called a dragger) is a fishing boat that can come in many different shapes and sizes. It catches fish by dragging fishing nets, called trawls, behind it.

FLAG LETTER:

U

FLAG NAME:
UNIFORM

FLAG MEANING:

YOU ARE RUNNING INTO DANGER.

The UNIFORM flag is one way to tell ships they need to be careful. Today, most ships send out sound signals or radio communication to let another boat know that they are running into danger. But the UNIFORM flag is often hoisted by someone on shore to warn boats of hidden dangers in the water, like rocks or shallow areas.

In foggy conditions, when ships can't see the shore (or a flag on shore), sound signals are often used to send the UNIFORM signal. The Morse code for UNIFORM is two short tones and one long tone, and it can be sent by sound or light.

OTHER NAUTICAL CODES FOR THE LETTER "U"

PHONETIC ALPHABET

UNIFORM

UNIFORM is pronounced you-nee-form. Other military and phonetic alphabets have used Uncle.

MORSE CODE / SOUND AND LIGHT SIGNAL

Make two short tones and one long tone with equal space between them.

SEMAPHORE

Hold both arms beside you and upward at a diagonal.

ABOUT FERRY BOATS

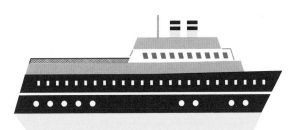

A ferry boat can be big or small, fast or slow. It carries passengers, cars and goods over short distances, and usually runs on a regular timetable, like a bus.

V

FLAG MEANING:

I REQUIRE ASSISTANCE.

The VICTOR flag is not a distress signal like NOVEMBER, CHARLIE or SOS, so it is never used to signal danger, but it is hoisted when a boat needs help with something that is less of an emergency. For example, if a ship has had a complete power failure and cannot communicate by radio, it may need the help of another boat's radio to help communicate with its owners, so that help can be sent to repair it.

OTHER NAUTICAL CODES FOR THE LETTER "V"

PHONETIC ALPHABET

VICTOR

VICTOR is pronounced vik-tah. Other military and phonetic alphabets have used Vinegar and Vic.

MORSE CODE / SOUND AND LIGHT SIGNAL

Make three short tones and one long tone with equal space between them.

SEMAPHORE

Hold your right arm straight up over your head and your left arm out beside you at a downward diagonal.

ABOUT COMMERCIAL YACHTS

A commercial yacht is bigger than other yachts, and can be chartered, or rented, by people who'd like to use it for competitive fishing, travel or fun.

FLAG LETTER:

W

FLAG NAME:
WHISKEY

FLAG MEANING:

I REQUIRE MEDICAL ASSISTANCE.

For passengers not used to sailing on a ship, a little seasickness is a common thing. But when someone gets seriously ill or injured, it's much more worrying. This is where the WHISKEY flag comes in. This flag tells other ships that there is an ill or injured person on board and that help is needed. If a ship is in harbour and medical assistance is on the way, the WHISKEY flag is hoisted to help make the ship easy to find.

A ship's crew can receive important medical instructions using a radio while they wait for help to arrive, but when the people speak different languages, a special medical code is used. Each message in the Medical Signal Code is made up of three flags: the MIKE flag and two other letters. These instructions help the crew tend to a patient when a doctor isn't available.

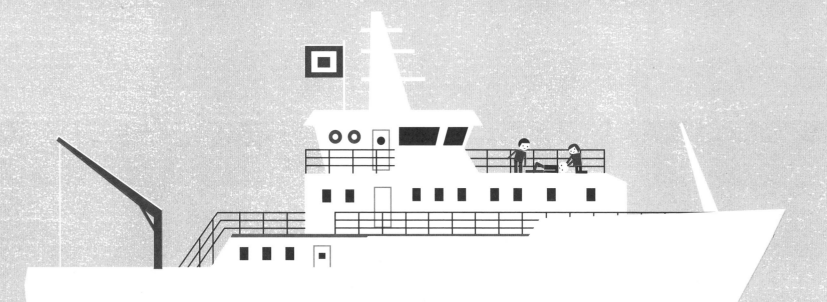

OTHER NAUTICAL CODES FOR THE LETTER "W"

PHONETIC ALPHABET

WHISKEY

WHISKEY is pronounced wiss-key. Other military and phonetic alphabets have used Willie and William.

MORSE CODE / SOUND AND LIGHT SIGNAL

Make one short tone and two long tones with equal space between them.

SEMAPHORE

Hold your left arm out beside you at an upward diagonal, with your right arm crossed over your front and straight out under your left arm.

ABOUT RESEARCH VESSELS

A research vessel comes in many different shapes and sizes and is specially designed for studying different parts of the ocean such as the ocean floor, sea water or sea life.

X

FLAG MEANING:

STOP CARRYING OUT YOUR INTENTIONS AND WATCH FOR MY SIGNALS.

Freeze! Halt! Stop what you are doing! The X-RAY flag is like saying all of that at once. But it doesn't just mean stop, it means stop and LISTEN to instructions. The X-RAY flag can be raised when a harbour boat notices that a ship is doing something wrong or dangerous. It can also be used to let a boat know that it is anchoring in a bad spot. It is usually followed by a signal with further directions.

OTHER NAUTICAL CODES FOR THE LETTER "X"

PHONETIC ALPHABET

X-RAY is pronounced ecks-ray. Other military and phonetic alphabets have used Xerxes, which is pronounced zurk-sees.

MORSE CODE / SOUND AND LIGHT SIGNAL

Make one long tone, two short tones and one long tone, with equal space between them.

SEMAPHORE

Hold your left arm out beside you at an upward diagonal, with your right arm crossed over your front and out beside you at a downward diagonal.

ABOUT RESCUE BOATS

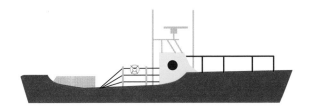

A rescue boat is specially equipped to help find and rescue anyone in danger at sea. Some rescue boats are on standby, which means that they are always ready, like fire engines, so that they can move quickly when called in to help.

FLAG LETTER:

Y

FLAG NAME:
YANKEE

FLAG MEANING:

I AM DRAGGING MY ANCHOR.

The YANKEE flag is raised when a boat is dragging its anchor – which is not a good thing! Ships drop their anchor when they want to stop moving. But when there are storms or strong winds, the force can be so powerful that the weight of the anchor and chain isn't enough to keep the boat still. That means that the boat begins moving again, but with its heavy anchor being dragged behind!

It can take quite a while to stop a dragging anchor, and it can cause serious accidents. So the YANKEE flag is hoisted when sailors want to warn others that their boat and anchor are moving out of control.

OTHER NAUTICAL CODES FOR THE LETTER "Y"

PHONETIC ALPHABET

YANKEE

YANKEE is pronounced yang-kee. Other military and phonetic alphabets have used Yellow, Yorker and Yoke.

MORSE CODE / SOUND AND LIGHT SIGNAL

Make one long tone, one short tone and two long tones, with equal space between them.

SEMAPHORE

Hold your right arm out beside you at an upward diagonal, and your left arm straight out beside you.

ABOUT CABLE LAYERS

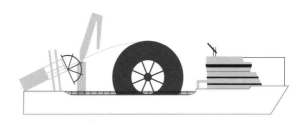

A cable layer lays down fibre-optic cables deep on the ocean floor, stretched out over very long distances. These cables carry telephone and Internet wiring, so that people around the world can be connected!

Z

FLAG MEANING:

I REQUIRE A TUG or I AM SHOOTING NETS.

This flag is special because it has two meanings, depending on who's flying it. When the ZULU flag is hoisted by fishing boats, it means that the boat is shooting fishing nets out into the water. Fishing nets can be several miles long, and can get caught in the engines of other boats, so it's important for other boats to stay away!

When the ZULU flag is hoisted by other ships, it means that they are unable to move and need another boat to help them

back to harbour. A ship might need to be towed (or "tugged") if its engine is down, or if it is a sailboat with no wind.

When used with the B flag to read BRAVO ZULU, this special naval code means "Well Done!" This message is generally sent by raising flags or by saying the words over radio. And since right now you've made it to the end of the flag alphabet, here's a special BRAVO ZULU to you!

OTHER NAUTICAL CODES FOR THE LETTER "Z"

PHONETIC ALPHABET

ZULU is pronounced zoo-loo. Other military and phonetic alphabets have used Zebra.

MORSE CODE / SOUND AND LIGHT SIGNAL

Make two long tones and two short tones with equal space between them.

SEMAPHORE

Hold your left arm straight out beside you, and your right arm in front of you at a downward diagonal under your left arm.

ABOUT CAR CARRIERS

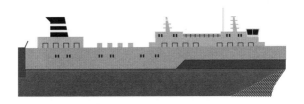

Car carriers are giant ships equipped with special ramps that allow cars to drive on and off. Some car carriers can carry thousands of cars to other places, where they can be sold.

INTERNATIONAL CODE of SIGNALS

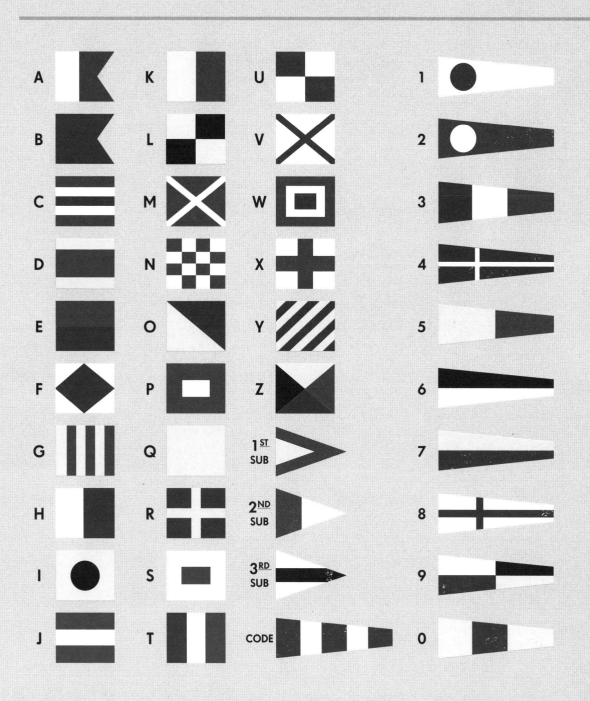

The **International Code of Signals** has forty signal flags in total — twenty-six **alphabet flags**, ten **numeral flags**, three **substitute flags** that are used when a letter or number is repeated, and one **code flag** that is used to signal that a message is coming or has been received. Sailors from around the world can communicate with one another using the International Code of Signals, even if they don't speak each other's language! This is why the United Nations International Maritime Organization (the IMO) requires all ships to carry signal flags, as well as a copy of the International Code of Signals.

SEMAPHORE

PHONETIC ALPHABET

ALPHA	ECHO	INDIA	MIKE	QUEBEC	UNIFORM	YANKEE
BRAVO	FOXTROT	JULIET	NOVEMBER	ROMEO	VICTOR	ZULU
CHARLIE	GOLF	KILO	OSCAR	SIERRA	WHISKEY	
DELTA	HOTEL	LIMA	PAPA	TANGO	X-RAY	

MORSE CODE

MORE ABOUT: NAUTICAL HISTORY

Naval fleets (groups of naval ships that are working on the same side) often create secret signal codes just for their own fleet so they can communicate without the enemy knowing. In the past these codes were kept in heavy, lead-covered books, so that if a ship were attacked, the top-secret codes would sink to the ocean floor and be safe from the enemy!

If you want to learn more about the history of signal flags, or more about nautical history in general, visit your local maritime museum, library, or with an adult's help, visit these websites:

www.history.navy.mil/research/library/exhibits/selection-of-signal-books.html

encyclopedia.kids.net.au/page/se/Semaphore_(communication)

www.seaflags.us/signals/Signals.html

www.crwflags.com/fotw/flags/xf~sfh.html

MORE ABOUT: CODES

The signal flags in this book are codes for some of the most common and urgent messages at sea, but they can also be combined in twos and threes to send more complicated messages. There are actually thousands of messages that can be communicated with these same flags!

If you would like to learn more about the other messages in the International Code of Signals, or more about the other codes and ships in this book, visit your local library, or with an adult's help, visit these websites:

www.riseacadets.org/training/phoneticalphabet.html

http://www.kidzsearch.com/wiki/NATO_phonetic_alphabet

http://morse-code.org/

http://www.seasources.net/PDF/PUB102.pdf

MORE ABOUT: DECORATING WITH FLAGS

Signal flags are also used to decorate ships. This is called "dressing a ship", and is often done on naval ships for special events such as celebrations, anniversaries and boat races, like you can see on the title page of this book!

If you want to learn more about how to use signal flags as decoration, here is some great inspiration! With an adult's help, visit these websites:

www.pinterest.com (create an account for free and search under "signal flags")

http://www.gettysburgflag.com/blog/flag-information/dressing-ships/

MORE ABOUT: BOATS

Did you know that shipping is one of the oldest jobs in the world and it's still a very important job? Around 90 per cent of the world's goods are transported across the sea by ships today!

If you would like to learn more about boats and shipping, visit your local maritime museum, library, read *Visual Encyclopedia of Ships* by David Ross, or with an adult's help, visit these websites:

www.imo.org (children's site coming soon!)

boatsafe.com/kids

www.nautinst.org

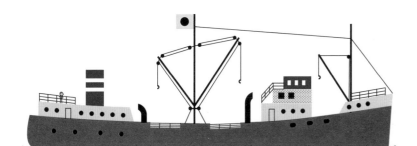

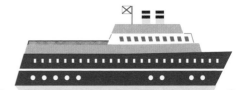

GLOSSARY of NAUTICAL WORDS:

Aboard – To be on or in a vessel.

Affirmative – Another way to say yes.

Anchor – A heavy object attached to a chain or rope that is dropped from a boat or ship to stop the vessel from moving.

Bow – The front end of a boat or ship.

Cargo – The goods carried by a ship.

Captain – The leader in charge of a ship.

Crew – The people who work on a ship.

Dock – A raised platform that is built out into the water so boats can load and offload their cargo.

Docking – To bring a boat into a dock or landing area.

Harbour – A place where ships can shelter from the weather and that is deep enough to drop anchor.

Horizon – The line where water (or land) meets the sky.

Hull – The part of a boat that sits underwater.

International Code of Signals – A worldwide system of codes that vessels can use to communicate with each other.

Lifeboat – A small boat that is used to get the crew to safety if something happens to the mother ship.

Manoeuvre – To skilfully move a ship.

Medical Signal Code – A system of signals used to give medical help to those on ships without doctors.

Morse code – A code used for sending messages where each letter of a word is represented by a series of short or long sounds or flashes of light.

Navigation lights – The lights on a vessel that are used to show its position when it's dark or foggy.

Negative – Another way to say no.

Phonetic Alphabet – A system of code words for each letter of the alphabet that is used by people who send messages so that similar-sounding letters are not confused.

Pilot – A specially trained sailor who can steer large vessels through difficult waters and busy harbours.

Port – The left-hand side of the ship when facing forwards, or, a harbour town or city where ships can dock.

Propeller – The blades on a ship that spin around to make it move.

Propulsion – A force that makes something move.

Quarantine – Keeping people who have a disease away from others to stop the illness from spreading.

Reef – A line or ring of rocks or coral near the water's surface.

SCUBA – A device that lets a diver breathe underwater.

Semaphore – A signalling system where a person holds a flag in each hand and changes the positions of their arms to spell out messages.

She – The way sailors refer to boats.

Signal flag – A signalling system where each unique flag is used to represent a different letter of the alphabet.

Signal (or blinker) lamp – A lamp used to send light signals – usually in Morse code – by opening and closing shutters in front of the lamp so that the light can be flashed on and off quickly.

Starboard – The right-hand side of the ship when facing forwards.

Stern – The back end of a boat or ship.

Vessel – A big boat or a ship.